Return to the Hinterlands
*more travels
around England's non-league football grounds*

Enjoy
Tawes
"Come on Chorley"!

Published in Great Britain in 2024
by Big White Shed, Morecambe, Lancashire
www.bigwhiteshed.co.uk
Printed and bound by Imprint Digital, Devon

ISBN 978-1-915021-33-5
Copyright © Christopher Towers
Cover Design & Illustrations by Robert Lever (www.leverart.co.uk)

The rights of Christopher Towers to be identified as the author of this work has been asserted in their accordance with Copyright, Designs and Patents Act of 1988, all rights reserved.

A CIP catalogue record of this book is available from the British Library.

Introduction

Welcome to another volume of 'Hinterlands' and more travels around England's non-league football grounds in poetic fashion with, as in the first edition, twenty-four games.

The book is about more than just football. It's about people and places across the country, reflecting the diversity of the non-league game but also the diversity of people and place. The first poem takes you to a late summer's day on the Wirral watching a team, Vauxhall Motors, associated with the car industry. We finish the following April when Smethwick Rangers (formerly called 'Smethwick Sikh Temple'), played Hinckley AFC. It was good to be 'back' - for the last 'Hinterlands' was written during the pandemic and featured games all played before Covid 19 hit these shores. In fact, the first poem in this book celebrates the togetherness of people at that match in the Wirral. From there it has been another journey around England's industrial and often post-industrial landscapes and to other places, other kinds of 'Hinterlands', from a public house team in Newark upon Trent to FC Romania in Cheshunt, to the Welsh borders and Dover. There is a women's match in Nottinghamshire, as the thriving women's game is represented in a non-league context. My search for more diversity than in the earlier edition of 'Hinterlands' has often involved hotel stays, all in the name of poetry, but more than that, to give voice and recognition to places and teams given little or no coverage by mainstream media. And unlike last time, the games are all played in one season, 2023-24, with all the vagaries of the weather and the different moods of seasons.

My monthly poetic match reports for 'The Non-League Paper' usually involve rhyme and of course this suits football. Games do evoke melodies, with fans chanting, often in waves. Sonnet and villanelle and other such forms can suit games and places and I use these forms in other contexts or on other platforms. The poems for this book are all however, written, as in the first volume, in free verse, without any rhyming scheme. I wanted again to write stories in loose poetic form, with more freedom to express. I take my notebook and scribble anything that comes to mind and take in all the senses. I need readers to 'see' the grounds but also listen to the sounds, from conversations, to the sounds of nature and the game itself. My poem about the Coventry Sphinx game versus Sporting Khalsa in August focused on those conversations. The poem, titled 'Watching' is about more than watching, it is about listening and, unlike in the professional game, the crowds can be small enough to hear everything. Sometimes the crowds are so small one can hear amazing sounds. I was listening to the carillon bells of the local church when watching Cadbury Athletic play on their Bourneville ground.

I took my notebook and pen and often sat in places that encourage observation, such as where the press sits, listening to the commentaries and 'with' referees' assessors, notably at Vauxhall Motors, with a very knowledgeable representative of the Football Association who was sitting there observing the referee's every move. There have been many themes, and one notable one has been ground ownership. Many of the teams and clubs play on land that has been contested in some way or subject to the politics of real estate. Visiting Wakefield on a sunny autumn afternoon, I was aware that their ground is shared with the Rugby League Club. The same could be said when visiting Newark and Sherwood in Nottinghamshire. This vegan club were moved out of Newark Town some years back and remain nomadic, desperate to get back to their roots. And then there was FC Romania, sharing the ground with Cheshunt, but again they are renters, the junior partner in the arrangement. There was also the issue of identity. FC Romania may bear the name of a country and indeed wear their national strip, but the team has no more than one player from Romania. Most of the original Romanian nationals who make up that team, they were formed in 2006, left the country when the United Kingdom left the European Union. My trip to New Saints versus Bala Town in the autumn was a curious one, for New Saints, although playing in the Welsh Premier League, play their matches in England, at a ground just outside Oswestry. I had great problems finding the place, tucked away off a motorway.

Then there are the hinterlands of time. Not all games are played at the iconic 3pm on a Saturday afternoon. I went to a youth match at Basford in Nottinghamshire on a Wednesday afternoon when people are usually earning a 'crust'. It was for an under nineteen game, played in front of a few supporters. I took my trusty notepad to the game and in the quietness observed the young teams moving the ball with some finesse in front of eager coaches. These places and times also lend themselves to poetry as I found myself observing the nearby houses and the Nottingham tram. Indeed, the streets were very close at a game in Merseyside when Marine played Bradford Park Avenue. This game was played at a ground, Rossett Park, overlooked by back gardens and patios. The game was literally close to people as I sat high in the stand, a guest of this wonderful club. The professional game is so far from the people in so many ways, but here I could not have been closer to the players and the pitch.

My games last time, in the first volume of 'Hinterlands', did not feature a Sunday football match but I thought I would change all that with a visit to a game in Newark, Nottinghamshire featuring a pub team 'The Duck' and a team with historic church connections, 'Holy Trinity'.

'Trinity' was, once upon a time, made up of Catholics, with the team representing a Catholic Church in the town. Again, we have club history linked to other aspects of social life, and indeed another of the teams featured, Stafford Rangers were allegedly started with the formation of a Bible class. Many of my poems reminisce or at least reflect some themes of 'yesterday' and how things change or perhaps stay the same. My trip to Enfield Town in the spring evoked times past. This was the case when watching this Fenix Trophy game, a kind of Champions League for non-league. Enfield play in a delightful Art Deco style ground, the main stand is rather classical with a circular café, which is a bar, with brickwork of the period. The game had a rawness, and a friendliness that I will never forget. Their opponents, Llantwit Major from Vale of Glamorgan, played with a real spirit. I made many notes before composing the poem 'Enfield'.

I tend to write the poems over days, from notes to first draft and then other drafts. I write when the ideas come, often late at night. I recall phrases, images, and sounds and seek to craft them into a poem. It is a labour of love. I love words and poetry and I love non-league football, the two marry together. There are themes to explore and stories to tell and this collection tells them. The game is close to people and the words are never far away. Many of the supporters speak words that are poetic themselves, even if they don't know it. Many of us are poets really, it's just not always recognised.

11 We're Back
Vauxhall Motors v Witton Albion
August 12th 2023

13 Watching
Coventry Sphinx v Sporting Khalsa
August 22nd 2023

15 Lullabies in the Sun
Sandiacre Town v Hucknall Town
August 26th 2023

17 White Shirts
Stafford Rangers v Marine AFC
September 9th 2023

19 That Night
Heanor Town v Saffron Dynamo
September 27th 2023

21 In the Side Streets
Wakefield AFC v Ollerton Town
October 14th 2023

23 Borderlands
New Saints v Bala Town
October 28th 2023

25 Homeless
Newark and Sherwood United v Carlton Town
November 7th 2023

27 Tears for Teversal
Newark Town Ladies v Teversal Ladies
November 19th 2023

29 Like the First Time
Worksop Town v Marine AFC
November 25th 2023

31 Beyond the Baubles
Tamworth v Buxton
January 6th 2024

33 Mundane
**Basford United U19
v AFC Rushden & Diamonds U19**
January 17th 2024

35 Salt and Pepper
Goole AFC v Silsden AFC
January 27th 2024

37 Sunshine over Grimsby
Grimsby Borough v Ashington AFC
February 10th 2024

39 I'll Remember
**Hinckley Leicester Road
v AFC Rushden & Diamonds**
February 17th 2024

41 Slumbers in Grantham
Grantham Town v Dunston UTS
February 20th 2024

43 From the Shed
Marine AFC v Bradford Park Avenue AFC
February 24th 2024

45 The Last Sandcastle
Dover Athletic v Maidstone United
March 2nd 2024

47 Sunshades and Smiles
Carlton Town v Stockton Town
March 9th 2024

49 Sons and Mothers
The Duck v Holy Trinity FC
March 10th 2024

51 Bourneville
Cadbury Athletic FC v Alcester Town
March 16th 2024

53 Enfield
Enfield Town v Llantwit Major
March 19th 2024

55 Theobalds Lane
FC Romania v Cockfosters
March 20th 2024

57 At Home
Smethwick Rangers v Hinckley Leicester Road
April 20th 2024

Vauxhall Motors 2 Witton Albion 2
Northern Premier League West Division
Saturday, August 12th 2023

The vanEupen Arena,
Ellesmere Port, Cheshire, CH66 1NJ

The club was established in 1963, after the opening of the new car plant. Situated in Hooton, next to the Ellesmere Port golf course.

We're Back

I recall the orange shirts of Witton,
as bright as lollies on the beach,
and the swirling wind, as if driven
by giant hair dryers in the sky.

I swear I smelled seaside salt,
circling around you, twirling
in the air and felt it in my nostrils,
tickling the skin.

It was good to be here again,
to talk with you and see you,
not an image on a static screen,
as when on pandemic days,

we yearned for touch,
and connection.
That's why we came here,
to this place, near a car factory.

Your face, bathed in rays of light,
speckling your cheeks.
Three years have passed since those
days of Covid briefings,

armchair leather and tea
and biscuit trails.
This game was like footie
between wind-breaks,

but it didn't matter,
with your smile as bright as
toffee apples and the
wind in your hair.

Coventry Sphinx 0 Sporting Khalsa 1
Northern Premier League Midlands Division
Tuesday, August 22nd 2023

The Sphinx Industrial Supplies Arena, Sphinx Drive, Coventry, West Midlands, CV3 1WA

Established in 1946 as a works team for Armstrong Siddeley, under the name of Armstrong Siddeley Football club. They adopted their current name, 'Sphinx', in 1960.

Watching

"The ultra-scan was alright," she said,
behind a blue and yellow scarf.
 "He's been teaching in France,"
said another, with a smile to the side.

"The sun is setting over Coventry,
it looks like a fire in the sky,"
one said, passing the stand,
walking like a duck.

 "There's a tropical storm in Texas,
it's the hurricane season you know,"
said one, with knees shaking, like
a washer at the end of its cycle.

 "It's good to be seeing you,"
said one to another as the cars
in the car park growled their
engines, like angry dogs.

"Been on your hols", one said,
straining his eyes in the sun.
"Sphinx is a cat" said a man with
a dog, rolling eyes to the sky.

'The piles are agony," he said
with fixed eyes, shuffling around
on his seat, "we must go
and watch a game".

Sandiacre Town 1 Hucknall Town 5
FA Vase
Saturday, August 26th 2023

Stanton Road, Sandiacre, Nottingham, NG10 5DE

The club house was built in 1982 at a cost of £40,000 and club members raised half the monies. It was completed in 1984, with the support of the Manpower Services Commission.

Lullabies in the Sun

Nylon shorts covered wide girths
in the sunshine, as spectators
mingled in a gaggle by pitch side,
leaning upon railings in the sun,
standing by it as if it was the bar
in a seaside public house.

Their t-shirts billowing in winds,
with cigarette butts hanging
from mouths like autumn
leaves about to fall, with smoke
winding its way over the
trees to the town.

Players waddled around
the pitch as if on beach side
pebbles, hot from the sun.
But Hucknall found rhythm,
rolling the ball into netting
five times, only stopping
to suckle plastic bottles,
gorging on water.

Trees swished their leaves,
lingering on their branches,
as summer lost its lustre.
Parents coddled their babies,
jigging them in their arms,
with lullabies in the sun.

Stafford Rangers 0 Marine AFC 2
Northern Premier League Premier Division
Saturday, September 9th 2023

**The Stan Robinson Stadium,
Marston Road, Stafford, ST16 3BX**
There are different theories on how and when the club was formed, but one such theory is that it was started by a Bible class.

White Shirts

I never yearned for a desk job,
wearing masks of compliance,
with offices open plan, coffee
clubs, niceties, and biscuits.

With uniform and spruced hair,
shoeshine, scrubbed faces
and shirts as buttoned as
their emotions.

And yet, here sat the officials,
in white shirts with clipped ties,
bearing the crest of the club,
for Rangers, to whom I serve.

Sitting with ironed creases,
with cuff-linked silver and badges
for lapels to sparkle on the white.
Marine were muscular and too

good for the men in white shirts,
twitching with anxiety as they sat
knee to knee, high in the stand,
in the fading September sun.

The players passed, then moved,
with overlap and runners waiting,
in weather too warm for it.
And as the white shirts rose from

their seats in an orderly fashion,
they remembered why they serve.
Not for mortgage, but for the club,
for the town, and more days in the sun.

Heanor Town 2 Saffron Dynamo 4
United Counties League Cup
Wednesday, September 27th 2023

Mayfield Avenue,
Heanor, DE75 7EN
The club was established in 1883 at a meeting at the Rays Arms Hotel.

That Night

I remember that night on our
rusty benches, sitting in the glare
of floodlights, in musty seating,
right behind the goal.

We sat with our metal flasks,
talking of hospitals and the long,
lost days down the pit and the life
you have lived since your fall.

We watched the play, half distracted,
on a night of cool, cross winds,
when we laughed about freight trains
still steaming through Heanor, with

make-believe jobs in our town.
But it was cold, as you sat, munching
pork scratchings, with the bag close
to your mouth,

shovelling them, as if your hand was
a spade. We said nothing as we watched
the goals being punched into the net,
too many times for Heanor.

You said something about saffron
being a herb, derived from the flower
of crocus. I smiled, then buttoned
my coat against the wind.

We could smell mushy peas and Bovril,
and I noticed your eyes fill.
We lived our dream at the club that
night and everything was what it was.

Wakefield AFC 11 Ollerton 0
Northeast Counties Football League Premier Division
Saturday, October 14th 2023

Belle Vue,
Doncaster Road, Wakefield, WF1 5EY

The team was originally based in the village of Emley and known as Emley AFC. The ground is shared with the Rugby League side Wakefield Trinity.

In the Side Streets

The side streets smelled of chip
lard and vinegar and grease upon
the papers. Of old mattresses, oils,
wheelie bins and pungent alleyways.

The places you can expect to find
old cookers, and discarded dressers.
Instead, you find a stadium painted,
patchy, peeling, and rusty.

A place for poets and priests,
for the soul and the soulless,
and those down on their luck.
But on a bright grey-white day,

when autumn entertained
the sun, Wakefield cut swathes
through green shirted Ollerton,
who played, like puppets

with broken strings, as I yearned
for battered fish and mushy peas,
served in the cobbled streets,
from side street chippies.

New Saints 2 Bala Town 0
Welsh Premier League
Saturday, October 28th 2023

**New Saints FC, Park Hall,
Whittingham, Oswestry, Shropshire, SY11 4AS**
The ground is in England, even if the team plays in the Welsh Premier League.

Borderlands

It felt like a secret party.
You knew they wouldn't
find you here, tucked away
behind some tall trees,
in an enclave, off a carriage way,
where bracken smelt of cinnamon,
dusted with rain, as I came upon
the 'New Saints', down a track.

I saw the bulbs of floodlights,
in a clearing, on the outskirts
of Oswestry, in the borderlands,
home and yet away, like a hotel
room or a home of a sort.
Saints' green hoops on white shirts
dazzled in the drizzle, as I heard
accents of Welsh and Shropshire.

The rain plastered the pitch as
Bala, in blood red, fell to a sling
shot from the Saints as rain
found strength beating on the
plastic pitch, like marbles falling.
Then a second from a penalty,
as some supporters twirled old
wooden rattles in the torrents.

Newark and Sherwood United 0 Carlton Town 2
Notts Senior Cup, 2nd Round
Tuesday, November 7th 2023

Newark & Sherwood United, Station Road, Collingham, Newark, Nottinghamshire, NG23 7RA
The club is a vegan club and only serve such food at matches. Many of the squad adopt plant-based diets.

Homeless

The home team are homeless.
Dumped from their hometown
by developers dreaming of assets

and homes far from where Newark
play, here in Collingham,
where the town rises with dawn,

when birds find their voice,
wagons roll and people stir
from their slumbers, in haste.

The team nestles in rurality,
with a pitch as bobbly as porridge,
and wobbly as cobble stones.

Floodlights sparked like an arc weld,
lighting the skies with their fires,
as Carlton, down from the smoke

of city life, dazzled in their shirts
and shorts of yellow, bright, and blue.
Their goals, more poached than eggs,

before referees' whistles made sirens,
as Newark trudged to their showers,
shirtless shame, and a dressing down.

Newark Town Ladies 12 Teversal Ladies 0
Nottinghamshire Girls and Ladies Football League
Seniors, Division One
Sunday, November 19th 2023

YMCA Activity village, Lord Hawke Way, Newark, Nottinghamshire, NG24 4FH
The ground resides within a housing estate and is next to the Leisure Centre and YMCA sports village.

Tears for Teversal

The ground sits in Lord Hawke Way,
where show houses stand ready for newly-weds
with huge gardens and cocktail glasses and the
smell of grass, freshly mowed in spring.

But this was a day when cool chlorine perfumed
the air, drifting from the swimming pool as lawn
mowers were left standing in the still air,
as the grey curtains of November skies drifted

over the plastic pitch, speckled with black dust.
Autumn leaves gathered as gym friends walked
with kit bags to assuage the guilt of big plated
roast lunches, laden with gravy, to come.

Passes went astray like false miss-steps
in a waltz on a slippery ballroom floor.
Newark netted the ball with chips and charges,
hair a bobbing, with deftness of foot.

With dark and light blue shirts mottled with mud,
Newark twirled shots into Teversal netting,
with motions as smooth as the turbines farming
wind over the fields, beyond the ground.

The rain spit and spat as the players left the field
with dark clouds and mutterings, gestures
and faces pink with anger and Tears for Teversal,
in the rain.

Worksop Town 0 Marine AFC 1
Northern Premier League, Premier Division
Saturday, November 25th 2023

Windsor Food Service Stadium,
Babbage Way, off Sandy Lane, Worksop, S80 1UJ

The club was founded in 1861 to make it (allegedly) the fourth oldest association football club in the world.

Like the First Time

They were watching, with eager eyes,
new supporters to the non-league game,
in seats as yellow as that toy yellow
submarine their grandad talks about.

The pitch as green as that Subbuteo pitch,
recovered from the loft, and Worksop Shirts
as bright as the brightest lemons, picked
from the best of evergreen trees.

Dad said they normally watched Wednesday,
but was thrilled at the good thing they'd found,
like the first swirl of cream on a cornet
or sticky treacle, served in a tray.

As my friends walked away, the father
made a promise to his kids, to return.
He'd found the game again,
as if for the first time.

Tamworth 2 Buxton 0
National League North
Saturday, January 6th 2024

Tamworth, The Lamb Ground, Kettlebrook Road, Tamworth, Staffordshire, B77 1AA
The club are known as 'the lambs'. 'The Lamb Inn' public house used to stand where new houses now sit, near the entrance to the car park, off the Kettlebrook Road.

Beyond the Baubles

We queued for bangers and chips,
clasped the sauce bottle, squeezed it,
then sprinkled salt and vinegar so hard
it made the chips glisten on white
plastic trays as we huddled in muddy
patches and puddles of rain.

We funnelled hot chips into
mouths - on a day beyond the baubles,
tinsel, turkey, and tantrums.
The chip van glowed like a two bar
fire with its orange furnace, in a
ground with its red painted walls.

Tamworth wrestled the game away
from Buxton, tearing at the defence
like eager children, ripping paper
from gifts yet to be discovered
as, in the distance, birds gathered
on roof tops, in the gloom.

Basford United U19 0
AFC Rushden & Diamonds U19 2
National League Under 19 Alliance League Cup, 3rd Round
Wednesday, January 17th 2024

Basford United,
Greenwich Avenue, Nottingham, NG6 0LD
The club was formed at the old 'Pear Tree Inn' in 1900.

Mundane

I sat with teenagers, and those
with nothing better to do on a
Wednesday afternoon in January,
watching Basford in yellow shirts,

looking like retro sherbet fountains,
with long black jerseys underneath,
like the liquorice under wrappers,
billowing cotton in the wind.

Two early Rushden goals,
both bundled over the line,
bodies bump to bump,
like shopping trolley

skirmishes in a windy car
park, the ball, like a melon,
falling, and customers
surprised to see it there.

Each melee finished with
squeals from Rushden youth,
like excited whales or
dolphins finding fishy treats.

A linesman was gruff under
a beanie, perched on his head,
like a gnome
that had escaped a garden.

Rushden found a huddle
at the finish, arms locked,
in the round, as if gossiping
about the win.

Goole AFC 3 Silsden AFC 0
Tool Station Northeast Counties Premier League
Saturday, January 27th 2024

Goole AFC Marcus St,
Goole, DN14 6TN

The two water towers, known as the 'salt and pepper pots' tower over the ground and the town. They were given grade two listed status by English Heritage in 1987.

Salt and Pepper

You always loved the Salt and Pepper pots,
those aptly named water towers standing
over the town, yet always out of reach.

Brown and white monuments that graced
the land when you had acid stomachs,
coming home from school you'd glance at them.

One a tower, the other cylindrical, dirty white.
Now here you are, at the game, with those
towers watching over you, as before.

The teams played tug of war with the ball
and each other, wrestling control in mud,
as you smelled burger and onions.

Yellow topped Silsden looked like safety
wardens or lollipop ladies of your youth,
glowing in the fading light.

Grimsby Borough 1 Ashington AFC 2
Northern Premier League (East Division)
Saturday, February 10th 2024

**Bradley Football Development Centre,
Bradley Road, Grimsby, DN37 0AG**
The team nickname is 'the wilderness boys'. It's just eight minutes' walk from a pub called the Bradley Inn.

Sunshine over Grimsby

The air would have been as cold as a fish market,
had it not been for the sun shining over a quiet Grimsby
neighbourhood, far from the pier, sands, and the docks.

Suburbia was on the doorstep of the ground as a man
with greasy grey hair, swept back, walked a corgi dog
along the pitch as if he was heading to the newsagent.

Meanwhile olive shirted Ashington pranced up the pitch
as if scaling a snakes and ladders board, players moving,
into space in zig-zag motion, half forward and side.

Ashington powered two goals, slide rule precise,
balls nestling in nets like plums in a basket,
as the north east men beat out a tune

on the back of a stand, hammering hard
like angry metalsmiths, as their team
protected the ball like deer with their fawns.

The sun blessed the sky with streaks
of colour, strawberry blancmange
with watery milk, tinged with orange,
as the Ashington drum beat once more.

Hinckley Leicester Road 3
AFC Rushden & Diamonds 0
Midlands Division
Saturday, February 17th 2024

Leicester Road Stadium, Leicester Rd, Hinckley, Leicester, LE10 3DR
The club was formed in 2013 after Hinckley United went into liquidation.

I'll Remember

You'll ask me and I'll forget the rain,
falling like showers of vinegar spots,
dropping to a soggy chip tray or the
clouds, looking like wiry wool Brillo
pads upon an opaque sky.

And I will not recall the cars
on the Leicester Road moving fast
and hot like molten metal
or the blue and red striped shirts
of Hinckley, Barcelona in my dreams.

But I will recall the sound of singing
Rushden fans, with a lumped throat
at their emotion, with memories
of listening to seashells at school.
But this sound, sharper than seas,

louder than the ocean but softer
than a sigh, deeper than a baritone,
more passionate than a thousand
kisses, gentler than a breeze,
but with a verve to move me.

I will recall the yearning passion
in the sound of the rolling chant
and the voices of affection for
place and time, that echoed
oh, so gently around the stand.

Grantham Town 1 Dunston UTS 1
Northern Premier League East Division
Tuesday, February 20th 2024

Grantham Town, South Kesteven Sports Stadium, Trent Road, Grantham, NG31 7XQ

When a local baker mixed up the ingredients for Grantham Whetstones for gingerbread, it became so popular he continued to make it and the club got their nickname, the 'Grantham Gingerbreads'.

Slumbers in Grantham

With the floodlights
as dim as oil lamps and the
game as quiet as a milk float,
I felt like taking a nap.

Distant Tannoy speakers
echoed muffled messages,
the kind you hear at checkouts
in supermarkets.

It was time to observe a leisure
centre in the distance, looking
like a giant Perspex fronted
hamster cage, with tunnels.

Meanwhile, a ball was tossed
like a bone between the players,
moving like lame labradors
on leads, as the ball slipped

like loose soap in a bathtub,
before two goals woke fans,
like dogs, waking with a yawn
and a stretch by the fire.

Marine AFC 4 Bradford Park Avenue AFC 0
Northern Premier League Premier Division
Saturday, February 24th 2024

**Marine AFC, The Marine Travel Arena,
College Road, Crosby, L23 3AS**
Marine had the longest serving manager in the game, Roy Howard, who was in post from 1972-2005.

From the Shed

There was I, perching with squinting eyes,
watching with a sun too high for February,
up in the stand at Rossett Park.

Watching trains snake through side-streets
to Crosby Beach and Blundell Sands where
Gormley statues stand, looking at the sea.

Avenue defenders looked embarrassed
in their shocking red cheek of a kit, standing
like those statues as Marine scored goals.

A man watched the game from a garden shed,
the other side of high nets, to stop the ball
from entering their patios and dining rooms.

The houses so close you could almost order
toast from their kitchens to the stands,
and advise the managers and coaches,

watching Marine players blaze their way
like sky-writer's trails, running through
Bradford's defence, with flare.

I smelled sea air and the warmth from the
stands and noticed our man in the shed,
open another can.

Dover Athletic 0 Maidstone United 1
National League South
Saturday, March 2nd 2024

Crabble Athletic Ground,
Lewisham Road, River, Dover, Kent CT17 0QJ

Dover players are known as 'the whites' by their supporters because of their white strip.

The Last Sandcastle

The sea rolled around the Dover front,
moving like a giant quilt with a restless
man underneath, rolling and rolling,
and then slapping the sea walls.

Dover stood like the last sandcastle,
the last town before the channel
and the winds from France, ready
to be washed away, abandoned.

Container ships and check points
and old Art Deco buildings
stood with winds sweeping the
proms, bending umbrellas.

Boarded up shop fronts lined the
town with charity shops and men
dishevelled and hunting around
for scraps, like the seagulls.

A town where craggy union jacks
twirled around their poles in front
of bedsits for the homeless,
the lost and never was.

In a town squealing with white
feathered birds and cargo ships,
belching their sirens in the far
off waters in the channel.

Carlton Town 1 Stockton Town 2
Northern Premier League East Division
Saturday, March 9th 2024

The Bill Stokeld Stadium,
Stoke Lane, Gedling, Nottinghamshire, NG4 2QS

Founded in 1904 under the name 'Sneinton FC' - the club have played at many different grounds and only settled at Stoke Lane in the early 1990s.

Sunshades and Smiles

Stoke Lane was cradled in sunshine
as the traffic from the highways
breezed by, on a day for a good
sleep, in the warmth.

Warm beer rolled in glasses,
like waves slapping against harbour
walls as the men from Stockton
stood stoutly by the pitch.

Their team resplendent in black
and red squares, moved the ball
like wizards of pin and their goal
hit a post, in off, to the net.

Carlton flags were draped like
towels from the beach,
or as if hanging their laundry
to dry in the unfamiliar sun.

Stockton's winner made a
chisel of the scorer's head,
cut at an angle to the goal,
slanted to the right.

The Stockton goalie wished
Carlton fans well, with a shrug,
in the cooling winds, on a day
for sunshades and smiles.

The Duck 1 Holy Trinity 2
Sam Arnold Memorial Trophy (Semi- Final)
Sunday, March 10th 2024

Farndon Recreation Ground, Farndon, Newark, NG24 3TS

The Duck is a public house based in Newark, Holy Trinity is a Parish Football Club, historically linked to the Holy Trinity RC Church, in Newark.

Sons and Mothers

This was a morning for puffy pillows in bed
and radio clocks with some tea. For slippers
on carpets and flowers by the door and
sons choosing mum over football.

But here on a field like mushy mash,
and daffodils swaying in wind, the rain
spitter-spattered and sons took a soak
in the cold.

With black jackets and beanies and stoical
smiles, the kith and the kin lined the line.
The Duck needed beer and the Trinity a god,
as the ball was clumped forward.

Trinity scored with a stunner to net,
like a stone skimming across the sea and then
landing with a plop in the water, as the rain
lashed down upon the earth.

Trinity won it when their striker ran through
and the 'keeper dropped leather with shakes
in the wrists, as if holding a hot casserole dish,
without gloves.

Coaches glanced watches and shuffled
with umbrellas to hold off the soaking.
Time for sons, mothers, flowers of spring
and Sunday roasts, piping.

Cadbury Athletic 0 Alcester Town 0
Midland League First Division
Saturday, March 16th 2024

Cadbury Recreation Ground, 71 Linden Road, Bourneville, Birmingham B30 1LB

The club is not allowed to have floodlights installed as the heritage or conservation rules deem that it would not be in line with regulations and would change the nature of the village.

Bourneville

Fuelling memories of shiny silver paper,
cocoa powder infused the air as the bells
of carillon, played on an organ
in the church, rang out.

Their soft chimes rolled around the ground
in a place locked in time, an England
lost to many, with genteel tea shops
and lardy cake.

Cadburys played in chocolate wrapper shirts,
purple and swirly white to their bootstraps.
I thought of childhood and the first
Christmas stockings.

I recalled running fingers round wrappers
of chocolate favourites as the smells drifted
towards the dugouts, to the gatherings
of folk on moist, moss ridden steps.

The teams slugged it out with the Cadbury
'keeper stretching his torso wide with a leg
jutting out to save like a blade from a Swiss
army knife, flicked against a rising ball.

Balls were played to feet, but not always
the right ones, and the keepers clutched
the ball like kittens in control of wool,
clasping it high and low to all comers.

Meanwhile the carillon played on, chimes
ringing around the village as families
dribbled past the ground with their push
chairs, fresh from the Cadbury shop.

Enfield Town 3 Llantwit Major 2
Fenix Trophy Group A
Tuesday, March 19th 2024

Queen Elizabeth 2nd Stadium, Donkey Lane, Enfield, EN1 3PL

The ground was named after the Queen, crowned in 1952, and the ground was completed a year after, in 1953.

Enfield

I found you Enfield,
with your Art Deco stadium,
and circular café, with
its bold white lettering.

Your brown beige bricks and
royal blue rails and the dazzle
from your windows that made
me think of sparklers,

held in eager, nervous hands,
with their fizzing light
in darkness, smelling
charcoal and treacle toffee.

Your team, with purple shirts
as bright as a fireworks box,
sparkling with shimmy
shammy runs,

amid the crackle and cackle
of supporters, glowing
with songs of yesteryear,
reminding me of nights

when as a child we'd gather
in the chill of November,
huddling with potatoes
baking under orange hot fire.

You scored with a rocket,
rising high into the soft net,
so high I swear I saw smoke
billowing into the sky.

FC Romania 1 Cockfosters 1
Spartans South Midlands football league, Premier Division
Wednesday, March 20th 2024

The Stadium, Theobalds Lane, Cheshunt, Hertfordshire, EN8, 8RU

The club was formed in 2006 by some Romanian migrants to the UK.

Theobalds Lane

I will never forget Theobalds Lane,
in a quiet corner of Cheshunt,
down the road from Waltham Cross,
where the red buses ache with people.

I was looking for Romania, who play
in Cheshunt, down a winding path,
by a park, where crocus was budding
in earth.

A football team, making the town
its home in a Hertfordshire suburb
where children skipped, with their
heavy satchels, in the sun.

I remember the cold amid chards
of light twinkling through the trees,
bearing their first leaves of season,
fragile buds on young stems.

I remember the bright yellow shirts
of the Romanian team, as bright as
the first daffodils of spring, growing
by a hedgerow.

I recall my invite to the board room,
where I was served cakes shining with
sugar and tea in a generous urn,
served with care for a stranger.

They talked of the beginnings
of the club, on the endless fields
of Hackney Marshes, recalling
the first steps of a new life.

Smethwick Rangers 1 Hinckley Leicester Road 0
Midlands League Division One
Saturday, April 20th 2024

Church Road, The Royal Town of Sutton Coldfield, Birmingham, B73 5RY

Originally known as Smethwick Sikh Temple, the club have competed in the UK Asian football championships. Without a home ground in Smethwick, they are now sharing with Boldmere St Michaels, ten miles away.

At Home

Smethwick play in Boldmere,
sharing a 'home' in the suburbs far
from the grey of industry, a long way
from their roots.

A place where steel and steam engines
have turned their wheels, where saree
dresses grace the streets and the world
turns with industries old and new.

But Boldmere is now home, where
sunshine glows on tarmac and people
saunter to shops in socks and sandals
in the midday sun.

This is a place where rusty old and new
lawnmowers will churn sods of grass
or hover over lawns with stripes made
for Wembley on barley water days.

This game, as interesting as a paper jam
in a copier, watched over by singular
looking men picking at tight Cellophane,
wrapped around cobs,

as if peeling skin from their fingertips,
staring into space as the game groaned.
Smethwick won, a pass to a runner
stabbed into netting from the centre,

like a purposeful rubber stamp on books,
before the game blew away on a breeze,
and loose grass from nearby lawns drifted
in the air as spring took its turn.

About the Author

Dr Chris Towers is an innovative lecturer who has over the years used drama, film and indeed poetry to support his student learning. His innovative methods won him a major teaching award. He uses poetic expression and composes poems that draw from a lifetime of influences from a trip to Moscow just as communism had ended, to composing poems for German and Russian students when teaching safeguarding law and mental health overseas. He has honed his poetic craft and developed his awareness of poetry and how to work with it in the classroom through post graduate study at Nottingham Trent and Cambridge University. It is however his lifetime of experiences, including travel that are particularly significant. These range from journeys around non-league football grounds to working with words and poetry with refugees and works with poetry as a therapeutic method in health and social care. From meanderings through Singapore and Malaysia, from Sporting Khalsa in the suburbs of Wolverhampton to the banks of the Malacca River. He is poet of Sheffield FC, the oldest football club in the world, and writes for a national newspaper.